Starting Up
& Staying Sane

A Mental Health Survival Guide for Business Founders

By Matt Hymers

Contents

Dedicated to my Dad, Neil.
Without whose support, guidance and sacrifice I would never be able to even dream of doing what I've done in my career and tackling the challenges that lie ahead.

Introduction:

If you're embarking on the journey of starting and building a business or bringing an idea to life, I hope the following insights will be of use to you.

Starting a successful business is a challenge that cannot be fully comprehended until you are actually doing it. As someone who is currently in the midst of building a startup, I understand the physical, mental, and emotional toll it can take on you. There are moments where it feels like giving up is the only option.

I started writing this book during one of those moments of self-doubt, as a way to reassure myself and others going through the same struggles. It's often difficult to find people willing to openly discuss the challenges of starting a business, and we end up suffering in silence.

I cannot yet tell you whether my insights will come from the perspective of a successful or failed entrepreneur, as the line between the two is thin and constantly shifting. But I believe that regardless of the outcome, the lessons learned can be valuable.

The insights shared here are based on my own experiences, mistakes, and lessons learned. They are meant to serve as a reminder to keep pushing forward, even in the face of adversity. Starting a business can be unforgiving, frantic, and frightening, but it can also be incredibly rewarding and invigorating.

To all those out there working towards their goals, know that you are not alone. Keep going, one step at a time. This book is for you.

Thanks for Reading.

Matt

Look After Yourself

No matter how passionate you are about your business, it's important to remember that your health and well-being come first. This is not just a cliché; it's a fundamental truth that all business founders should keep in mind.

In the pursuit of success, it's easy to let important aspects of our lives slide. We may neglect our families, our sleep, our diet, and our fitness. We may convince ourselves that these things can wait, that we'll have time for them later, or that they are less important than our business goals.

But the truth is that neglecting these fundamental priorities can harm our chances of success. Poor sleep, a sedentary lifestyle, a bad diet, and neglecting our loved ones can lead to burnout, decreased productivity, and a general sense of dissatisfaction and unhappiness.

Taking care of your mental health and well-being is not an option; it's a necessity. You don't need fancy gadgets or a personal trainer to do it. Here are some simple steps you can take to prioritise your mental health and well-being:

1. Prioritize sleep: Aim for 7-8 hours of sleep every night. Make sure your sleeping environment is conducive to restful sleep, and avoid using electronic devices before bedtime.

2. Make time for fitness: You don't have to be a fitness guru to stay healthy. Even a 20-minute walk or a 15-minute yoga session can make a big difference in your physical and mental well-being.

3. Eat well: A balanced and healthy diet is essential for maintaining good physical and mental health. Avoid processed foods, limit your alcohol intake, and make sure to eat plenty of meat, fruits, nuts and vegetables.

4. Spend time with loved ones: Make time for your family and friends, and prioritize quality time with the people who matter most to you.

5. Prioritize quality time with loved ones: Don't neglect your relationships in the pursuit of success. It's important to make time for your family and friends, it's equally important to be present and engaged during that time. You don't need to be there for every single moment, but make an effort to be in the moment when you are with your loved ones. This means putting away your phone, listening actively, and showing genuine interest in their lives.

Prioritizing your mental health and well-being is crucial to your success as a business founder. By taking care of yourself, you'll be better equipped to tackle the challenges and opportunities that come your way. Remember, your family, sleep, health, fitness, and diet come first, and your business will benefit from your commitment to these priorities. While it may not be easy, it is simple.

Navigating Uncertainty

In the early stages of starting a business, it's common to feel like you're walking on the edge of a knife. Every decision you make seems crucial, and the slightest misstep could lead to failure. However, it's important to understand that success is rarely the result of a single stroke of good luck, and failure is rarely the result of one mistake.

Starting a business is a balancing act, and it's normal to feel like you're constantly teetering on the edge of success or failure. This can be incredibly anxiety-inducing, and you may experience a range of emotions, from feeling demoralized and depressed to feeling energized and optimistic. Sometimes, these feelings can change in the space of just thirty minutes.

It's crucial to learn to recognize, accept, and embrace these feelings. Instead of letting them overwhelm you, try to temper them back to a neutral state, and refocus on the tasks at hand and your ultimate vision.

One way to navigate the uncertainty of entrepreneurship is to focus on what you can control. Identify the areas of your business that are within your control, and work to improve them. For example, you can control how you communicate with customers, how you market your product, and how you manage your finances. By focusing on these areas, you can feel more confident and empowered, even in the face of uncertainty.

Another key to navigating the uncertainty of entrepreneurship is to stay adaptable. The business world is constantly changing, and you need to be able to pivot and adjust your strategy as needed. This means being open to feedback, willing to experiment and iterate, and being willing to make tough decisions when necessary.

It's also important to build a support network of mentors, advisors, and peers who can offer guidance, perspective, and support. Starting a business can be a lonely journey, and having a community of people who understand what you're going through can be incredibly valuable.

Starting a business is like riding a rollercoaster, going skydiving, or taking a leap of faith. Once you're on it, it's just a matter of taking the next step. The knife isn't as sharp or dangerous as it may seem, and success is rarely the result of one big win. Embrace the uncertainty, stay adaptable, and focus on what you can control, and you'll be on your way to building a successful business.

Mike Tyson Wisdom

Mike Tyson may seem like an unlikely source of wisdom for a mental health survival guide for business founders, given his troubled past and reputation as one of the most aggressive boxers of all time. But there are lessons to be learned from his life experiences that apply to everyday life and business.

Despite his flaws, Tyson has shared some powerful insights that have stood the test of time. These are my personal favorites that I've found to constantly ring true:

"Everybody you fight is not your enemy and everybody that helps you is not your friend."

This quote is a powerful reminder to be open-minded and not make assumptions about people's intentions. Along your journey, you will encounter people who you believe to be your allies, only to find out that they don't have your best interests at heart. Conversely, you may come across individuals who you initially dismissed, but who ultimately become valuable assets to your team. Keep an open mind and don't let your assumptions blind you to the reality of a situation.

"Everybody has a plan until they get punched in the mouth."

This quote speaks to the fact that life is unpredictable, and no matter how well you plan, things can still go awry. It's important to have a plan, but it's equally important to remain flexible and adaptable. Expect the unexpected and be prepared to pivot when necessary. Don't get too attached to your plans, as they may change at any moment.

Tyson's words can be applied not only to the world of business, but also to our personal lives. We all have plans and goals that we strive to achieve, but life has a way of throwing us curveballs when we least expect it. We must learn to be resilient, adaptable, and open-minded, just like Tyson did throughout his tumultuous life. Embrace the unpredictability of life and learn from the unexpected.

In summary, don't judge people too quickly and be prepared to pivot when life doesn't go according to plan. These are the lessons we can take from the infamous boxer, Mike Tyson.

Yin and Yang

Life and business are not all sunshine and rainbows. There will be moments of joy and success, but there will also be moments of pain and failure. As much as we try to avoid them, difficult times are inevitable. However, it is important to remember that every situation, whether good or bad, presents an opportunity for growth and improvement.

One of the fundamental principles of Taoism is the concept of Yin and Yang. Yin represents the negative or darker side of things, while Yang represents the positive or brighter side. The idea is that the two forces are interconnected and interdependent. Without one, the other cannot exist.

In life and business, there is always a balance between the positive and negative. Nothing is ever all good or all bad. A failure or setback may seem like the end of the world at first, but it can lead to valuable lessons and opportunities for growth. On the other hand, success may seem like the ultimate goal, but it can also bring unintended consequences or reveal areas for improvement.

It is important to approach both the positive and negative with a mindset of learning and growth. When things go wrong, take the time to reflect and analyze what went wrong and what can be done differently next time. Failure is not the end, but an opportunity to learn and grow. Similarly, when things go right, take the time to celebrate, but also evaluate what could have been done better and how to improve for the future.

In the moment, it can be difficult to see the positive in a negative situation or recognize areas for improvement in a successful one. However, with practice and mindfulness, it is possible to develop this skill. It is a mindset shift from seeing things as purely good or bad to recognizing the interconnectedness and interdependence of the two.

Embracing the Yin and Yang of life and business means accepting that challenges and surprises will come our way, but also recognizing that there is always something to be learned or gained from them. It means being open to the possibility of growth and improvement, no matter the circumstance. By embracing both the positive and negative, we can create a more balanced and fulfilling life and business.

Cash is King

Money makes the world go round. It's an age-old saying that is as true today as it ever was. But when it comes to entrepreneurship, the importance of cash cannot be overstated.

Cash flow is the lifeblood of any business. Without it, your business will wither and die. It's not just about having money, it's about having access to it when you need it the most.

Building a successful business is not easy. It takes hard work, persistence, and a bit of luck. Even then, success is not guaranteed. There are countless obstacles and roadblocks that you will encounter along the way.

One of the biggest challenges that every entrepreneur faces is managing cash flow. You might have a great product or service, a solid team, and a clear roadmap for growth, but if you don't have the cash to execute your plan, you're dead in the water.

Cash flow problems can arise from a variety of sources. It could be a delay in payment from a customer, a sudden increase in expenses, or a downturn in the economy. Whatever the reason, the effects can be devastating.

That's why it's important to be proactive and plan ahead. As an entrepreneur, you need to have a clear understanding of your financials. How much money do you need to get to the next stage of growth? How much runway do you have? What are your burn rate and cash flow projections?

It's not enough to just have a general idea of your financials. You need to get down into the details and have a clear plan for how you will manage your cash flow. This means having a budget and sticking to it, tracking your expenses and revenues, and constantly reviewing and updating your projections.

But even the best-laid plans can go awry. That's why it's important to have a contingency plan in place. This could mean having a line of credit or access to alternative sources of funding. It could also mean cutting expenses or pivoting your business model if things aren't working out.

At the end of the day, cash is king. Without it, your business will struggle to survive. As an entrepreneur, you need to make cash management a top priority. This means being proactive, planning ahead, and being flexible when things don't go according to plan.

So, get out there and build relationships with investors and customers. Share your vision and plans. Be transparent about your financials. And remember, cash is your lifeblood.

Find Wise Heads

When you're starting something new, it's easy to get caught up in the excitement and believe that you can handle everything on your own. But the truth is, no one can do it alone. You need the help and guidance of others who have been in your shoes before.

Finding wise heads - people who have the knowledge, skills, and experience to help you - is essential to your success. And the earlier you start looking for them, the better.

You might think that because you're doing something new and innovative, there's no one who has done it before. But the reality is that no matter what you're doing, there are always people who have done something similar. They may not have done it exactly the same way, but they have experience that can be valuable to you.

One of the biggest mistakes you can make is thinking you know everything. You don't. And if you try to go it alone, you're likely to make mistakes that could have been avoided. Wise heads can help you avoid those mistakes, and give you the guidance you need to succeed.

So how do you find these wise heads? Start by looking within your own network. Think about the people you know who have experience in your industry or who have started their own businesses. Talk to them about your plans and ask for their advice. You might be surprised at how willing they are to help.

But don't stop there. Expand your network by attending industry events and conferences. Look for people who are doing what you're doing, or who have experience in your field. Strike up a conversation and see if they would be willing to meet with you and share their knowledge.

And don't forget about the power of the internet. Social media platforms like LinkedIn and Twitter can be great tools for finding and connecting with people who can help you. Join industry groups and participate in discussions. You never know who you might meet or what kind of advice you might get.

When you do find wise heads, make sure you take their advice to heart. Listen carefully to what they have to say, and ask questions to make sure you understand. And don't be afraid to ask for more help if you need it.

In my own experience, I neglected the one person who was closest to me and who could have been a great source of wisdom: my Dad. I wish I had asked for his help earlier, but I was too caught up in my own ego to realize how much he could have helped me.

Don't make the same mistake. Find wise heads early, and take advantage of the knowledge and experience they have to offer. It could make all the difference in your success.

Embrace Being Clueless

It's an uncomfortable realisation, but the truth is that nobody truly knows what they're doing. We're all making educated guesses based on our experiences, knowledge, and skills. Even the most revered experts and successful individuals are still navigating through life by making their best guess.

It's up to you to evaluate and decide whether an opportunity is worth pursuing or not. Don't blindly follow someone's advice just because of their reputation or status. They may not see what you see, or they may be operating within their own limited sphere of knowledge and influence.

That being said, it's also important not to dismiss the advice and guidance of others. They may have valuable insights and perspectives that you haven't considered. Being open to different ideas and viewpoints can help you expand your own knowledge and understanding.

The key to success is being comfortable with being clueless. Embrace the uncertainty and take calculated risks. It's through making mistakes and learning from them that we grow and progress.

In fact, the most successful people are those who are constantly learning and adapting to new situations. They're not afraid to take risks and make mistakes, but they're also not too proud to seek help when they need it.

So, don't be afraid to ask questions and seek guidance from those around you. Build a network of wise heads who can offer different perspectives and expertise. But ultimately, trust your gut and take ownership of your decisions.

Remember, nobody has all the answers, and that's okay. It's through taking risks, making mistakes, and continuously learning that we can achieve our goals and become the best version of ourselves.

Chapter 8: Stop Obsessing Over the Competition and Focus on Your Business

It's easy to get caught up in what your competitors are doing. You may feel like you have to constantly monitor their every move and react to their actions. But the truth is, obsessing over your competition is a waste of time and energy.

Yes, it's important to keep an eye on your competition and be aware of what they are doing, but don't let it consume you. Your focus should always be on your business, your team, and your product.

Trying to outdo your competition at every turn is not only exhausting, but it also distracts you from what really matters – delivering value to your customers. You should be creating a product or service that solves a real problem and meets the needs of your target market.

Remember, you don't know the full story of what your competition is doing or why they are doing it. They may be making moves that don't make sense to you, but they could be part of a bigger strategy that you're not aware of. It's the same for them towards you and your business.

So instead of worrying about what your competition is doing, use their success as motivation to improve your own business. Look at what they are doing well and how you can apply those principles to your own operations. And if they're copying you, take it as a compliment and keep executing your strategy with confidence.

It's important to stay focused on your own goals and execute your plans to the best of your ability. Get feedback from your customers and use that to improve your product or service. Stick to your plan, stay committed, and success will come.

In short, stop obsessing over your competition and focus on your own business. Don't waste your time trying to outsmart or outmanoeuvre them. Instead, use their success as motivation to improve your own operations and deliver value to your customers.

Be You

Being yourself is a fundamental principle that applies to all aspects of life, including being a founder or CEO of a startup. There's no need to conform to a stereotypical archetype or put on a façade in order to fit in with the startup scene. In fact, being true to yourself can be a huge advantage.

Don't worry about what you wear, what you eat, or what kind of car you drive. Focus on what matters to you and your business. You don't need to attend every startup event or brown-nose your way through meaningless conversations. Instead, focus on the things that truly matter, like your team, your product, and your customers.

Success is built on blood, sweat, tears, and determination. You will make mistakes, but the key is to learn from them, celebrate your successes, and seize every worthwhile opportunity that comes your way. Be grounded and authentic, and don't apologize for being yourself. After all, it's your business, and you are as good, smart, and capable as anyone else on the planet.

Being authentic and true to yourself not only feels better, but it can also attract the right people and opportunities to your business. People are drawn to those who are genuine and passionate about what they do. When you are yourself, you attract the right kind of attention and build genuine relationships with customers, investors, and partners.

It's also important to remember that being yourself doesn't mean you can't grow and evolve. You can learn new things, develop new skills, and change your perspectives over time. The key is to stay true to your values and vision while remaining open to new experiences and opportunities for growth.

In conclusion, just be you. Don't try to fit into a mould or conform to someone else's expectations. Your unique perspective, personality, and experiences are what make you and your business stand out. Embrace your authenticity, and use it to your advantage.

Express yourself

In business, expressing yourself is crucial. It's essential to speak up about what you're feeling, as it can help those around you make informed decisions, ask the right questions, and find the best solutions to problems.

However, it's not always easy to be transparent about your feelings, especially if you're coming from a corporate background where office politics can be the norm. In such environments, every word you say can be used against you by a colleague or manager.

In your own business, your co-founders, investors, partners, employees, and service providers need to have a clear understanding of your thoughts and feelings, as they impact the company's overall atmosphere. If you're feeling frustrated, happy, angry, sad, scared, or excited, let them know, but in a controlled manner. Don't let your emotions get the best of you and lash out at people who make mistakes.

Assumptions can lead to misunderstandings, so it's important to communicate effectively. Speak up when something doesn't feel right, and be clear about what you want to achieve. This doesn't mean you should be overly aggressive or confrontational, but rather that you should find a way to convey your message clearly and respectfully.

Furthermore, expressing yourself is not just about sharing your feelings; it's also about being true to your values and beliefs. If something doesn't align with your values or mission, say so. Don't compromise your principles to please others or gain short-term advantages. Instead, stay true to yourself and

your business's vision, and let others know what you stand
for.

In conclusion, expressing yourself in business is crucial for
success. It helps everyone involved to make informed
decisions, understand where you stand, and work towards the
same goals. Don't be afraid to speak up and share your
thoughts and feelings, but do so in a respectful and controlled
manner. Be true to your values and vision, and let others
know what you stand for.

Communicate X 3

Communication is key in any business, but it becomes even more critical when you have co-founders, shareholders, customers, and other stakeholders involved. As a leader, it's your responsibility to communicate everything clearly, often, and to everyone involved in the business.

However, communication requires discipline and habit. You must develop a habit of communicating everything, from small events to major decisions, to everyone involved in the business. It's easy to let things slip through the cracks, but these little things can add up and lead to bigger problems down the road.

To stay on top of everything, you should aim to communicate at least three times more than you think you need to. This may seem like a lot, but it's better to over-communicate than under-communicate. It's important to record and talk about everything with the relevant parties regularly. This will help you stay on top of tasks, delegate effectively, and make progress towards your goals.

As a leader, it's your responsibility to communicate in a way that everyone can understand. You may have to adjust your communication style depending on who you're talking to. For example, if you're speaking with investors, you may need to use financial terminology to explain the financial health of the business. On the other hand, if you're speaking with employees, you may need to use simpler language to explain the company's goals and objectives.

Communication isn't just about talking, it's also about listening. As a leader, you need to listen to feedback from your team, customers, and stakeholders. This feedback can help you make better decisions and improve the overall quality of your business.

It's also important to be transparent with your communication. Be honest about the company's strengths and weaknesses, and share information openly. This will help build trust with your team and stakeholders.

Finally, remember that communication can be draining and tedious, but it's an essential part of running a successful business. Don't let important events or tasks slip through the cracks. Take the time to communicate effectively and regularly, and you'll set yourself and your business up for success.

Persistence through C.R.A.P.

Persistence is one of the key traits that sets successful entrepreneurs apart from those who fail. It's not just about having a great idea or being in the right place at the right time. It's about having the resilience and tenacity to push through the inevitable challenges and obstacles that come your way.

And there will be plenty of challenges and obstacles. You'll face **C**riticism from people who don't believe in your vision, **R**ejection from investors or customers, dealing with **A**ssholes who want to tear you down, and the constant **P**ressure of having to deliver results.

This is what I call C.R.A.P. It's the stuff that makes you want to quit, to throw in the towel and give up. But here's the thing: C.R.A.P. is everywhere, and you can't avoid it. You have to face it head-on and let it fuel you, not drain you.

The key is to persist through it all. You have to be unyielding, unwavering, and unending in your pursuit of success. Every mountain you climb has another waiting for you at the top. You'll fall down, get cut down, and face setbacks. But you have to get up, learn from your mistakes, and come back stronger, wiser, and better equipped.

The truth is, no matter where you are on your journey, there will always be more C.R.A.P. to deal with. But it's your ability to push through it again and again and again that will determine whether you come out the other side or not. The minute you stop, that's when you know it's over. You may get close to giving up a few times, but you have to keep going.

It helps to think of it like this: persist, because this CRAP will pass. It's a temporary obstacle that's just a small part of your journey. And in the end, it will make you stronger and better prepared to face whatever comes next.

So, embrace the C.R.A.P. and use it as fuel to keep pushing forward. Learn from it, grow from it, and let it propel you towards your ultimate goals. Because in the end, it's persistence that will get you there.

Trust Me...

Trust is the foundation of any successful business relationship. Without trust, it's hard to work towards a common goal, achieve desired outcomes, and build a thriving business. When you trust someone, you have faith that they will follow through on their commitments, deliver high-quality work, and work collaboratively towards shared goals.

However, trust is a two-way street. You can't expect others to trust you if you don't trust them. As a business owner, you need to be willing to delegate tasks and responsibilities to your team members and give them the autonomy to make decisions. You need to trust that they will make the right decisions and deliver quality work.

Of course, trusting others can be challenging, especially if you've been let down before. But it's important to remember that trust is built over time, through consistent actions and behaviors. You can start by setting clear expectations, communicating openly and honestly, and following through on your commitments. As your team members demonstrate their reliability and competency, you can gradually increase your trust in them.

It's also important to choose your business partners, investors, and vendors carefully. Look for people who share your values, have a track record of success, and communicate effectively. Conduct due diligence and ask for references before entering into any business relationships.

Ultimately, trusting others is about taking a leap of faith. It's about acknowledging that you can't do everything alone and that you need a team to help you achieve your goals. It's about recognizing that everyone has something valuable to offer and that together, you can achieve great things.

So, choose your team carefully, communicate openly and honestly, and give others the autonomy to make decisions and deliver results. Trust is the key to building a successful business, and it's something that needs to be nurtured and maintained over time.

Try Fly Fishing

In today's fast-paced world, where work seems to take up a significant portion of our lives, it's easy to become consumed by it. It's important to remember that there is more to life than work, and that we need to make time for other activities that bring us joy and fulfillment.

Having hobbies or other interests that are not work-related is essential for our well-being. They provide an opportunity to relax, recharge, and get our minds off work. Engaging in activities that we enjoy helps to reduce stress, improve our mood, and increase our overall happiness.

When it comes to choosing a hobby, it's important to pick something that we are genuinely interested in and that challenges us in some way. It should be an activity that we can't do while thinking about work, allowing us to fully immerse ourselves in the moment.

For me, my hobbies include exercise, painting, gardening, and occasionally fly fishing. These activities not only provide a much-needed break from work, but they also give me a sense of accomplishment and progress. When I'm painting or gardening, I'm creating something new and tangible, and that sense of accomplishment is incredibly rewarding.

It's important to note that hobbies or other activities should be productive and engaging. It's easy to fall into the trap of mindless activities such as binge-watching TV or scrolling through social media. These activities may provide a temporary escape from work, but they do not provide the same benefits as more productive activities.

Lastly, as an entrepreneur, it can be challenging to find time for hobbies or other activities. It's essential to make a conscious effort to prioritize these activities and schedule them into your day. By doing so, you'll not only improve your overall well-being but also enhance your productivity and creativity when you return to work.

In conclusion, having other things to do outside of work is crucial for our well-being and productivity. These activities should be productive, engaging, and challenging, providing an opportunity to relax, recharge, and get our minds off work. So go ahead, pick up a new hobby, and enjoy the benefits of doing other stuff.

Bye Bye Burnout

There is a common misconception in the startup culture that working non-stop is a badge of honour. But the truth is, constantly grinding away without taking breaks can actually be counterproductive and detrimental to your overall well-being.

Everyone has different limits, and there comes a point where pushing yourself to work harder and longer each day becomes futile. Even if you have a looming deadline or everything seems to be on the line, taking a break and coming back to it with a fresh perspective and renewed energy is often the best approach.

In fact, research has shown that taking short, power naps can be incredibly beneficial for productivity and creativity. If you're not sure how to power nap, take some time to learn and make it a regular part of your routine.

It's important to recognize when your mind and body are exhausted and your capacity to do good work is declining. This is the point where you need to step back and take a break. And if you absolutely need more time to finish a project, don't be afraid to communicate with your client or team and ask for an extension. More often than not, they will understand.

But taking a break doesn't mean indulging in unhealthy habits like binge eating or binge-watching TV shows. Instead, focus on doing activities that will help you reset and recharge, such as exercise, meditation, or spending time in nature.

Depriving yourself of sleep is also counterproductive and unhealthy. Getting enough rest is crucial for both physical and mental health. Make sure you prioritize getting adequate sleep each night to ensure that you are performing at your best.

Ultimately, it's about finding a balance between work and rest. When you find yourself grinding away, remember that taking breaks and prioritizing your mental and physical health is not only important, but essential for long-term success. Don't fall into the trap of the "hustle culture." Work smart, not hard, and take care of yourself along the way.

Think about it

In the fast-paced world we live in, taking time to think can seem like a luxury we can't afford. However, it's crucial for both personal and professional growth.

Making time in your schedule to do nothing but think can be purposeful and proactive. It allows you to digest the events of the past week and plan ahead. This time can be used to reflect on your accomplishments, evaluate your goals, and strategize for the future.

On the other hand, there are times when taking a step back and thinking is necessary. It's easy to get caught up in the day-to-day tasks and to-do lists, but sometimes situations can spiral out of control. In those moments, it's crucial to stop, step back, and reassess the situation.

When you're in the thick of things, it's imperative to take the time to step back, detach from the chaos of the everyday grind and assess the situation. This can help you identify potential solutions and avoid making rash decisions.

Furthermore, making time to think can also help you tap into your creativity and innovative ideas. It allows you to free your mind from distractions and explore new possibilities. You can use this time to brainstorm, write down your thoughts, and connect with your inner self.

Taking time to think is not a luxury, but a necessity for personal and professional growth. It's important to schedule time for proactive thinking and to recognize when it's necessary to take a step back and assess the situation. So, block off some time in your schedule, put away your phone, and start thinking!

Let it Go

Letting go of something that is bothering us can be one of the hardest things to do. It is in our nature to hold on, to ruminate, to worry, and to obsess. However, this behaviour only leads to more stress, anxiety, and negativity. I have a daughter who loves the Disney movie, Frozen, and the concept of letting go is beautifully articulated by Elsa, the main character who sings, you guessed it, "Let it go."

When something goes wrong, it is essential to acknowledge it, and then let it go. Don't dwell on it, don't make it bigger than it needs to be. Overthinking only amplifies the problem, turning it into a mammoth-sized issue.

This is not to say that we should ignore the problems or mistakes we make. It is essential to learn from them, analyse and understand them so we can improve. But once we have done that, we need to detach ourselves from the emotional charge that comes with it.

By letting it go, we free ourselves from the grip of negative emotions. We can be calm and objective, allowing us to focus on the solutions and the steps needed to move forward.

It's essential to understand that letting go is not the same as giving up. We need to accept that certain things are out of our control and work on what we can change. By letting go, we take back the power we need to move forward.

So, next time something goes wrong, or a mistake is made, take a deep breath. Understand the problem, learn from it, and then move forward with a clear and objective mind.

Letting go allows us to let it flow and move forward faster, feeling better and more in control of our lives.

Be like Elsa. Let it go.

Patience

Achieving success in any endeavour takes time, and patience is a virtue that should be cultivated. It's easy to feel like things are taking too long, whether it's sealing a deal, developing a product, or finding funding. However, it's important to remember that everything takes time, and pushing for instant results is not always the best approach.

Impatience can be a positive sign of one's drive and determination to succeed, but it can also wear down focus and make it difficult to stay on track. When we feel like things are not moving as fast as they should, it's important to re-focus on the things we can control.

For example, if you're waiting for a deal to close or for funding to come through, use that time to focus on the things you can control, such as improving your product or refining your business strategy. This can help move things along in the long run.

It's also important to remember that speed is critical in many situations, but there are some things that are beyond our control. When we feel like we're stuck in a holding pattern, it can be helpful to reframe our thinking and recognize that everything takes time.

By accepting that progress may take longer than we'd like, we can avoid getting bogged down in frustration and instead channel our energy into taking productive steps towards our goals. In the end, success is not just about getting to the finish line, but about the journey and the progress we make along the way.

Embracing Failure

The fear of failure is something that holds many people back from taking risks and pursuing their dreams. However, as the example of Nike's "Breaking2" project shows, failure is not something to be feared, but rather something to be embraced as a necessary part of the process.

In 2016, Nike attempted to break the two-hour marathon mark with their Breaking2 project, a three-year endeavor that was publicly broadcast. While they ultimately fell short by 25 seconds, the project was still a success in many ways. Nike had pushed the limits of what was thought to be possible in the sport, and had gained valuable insights and data that they could use in future endeavors.

The most impressive aspect of the Breaking2 project was the way in which Nike embraced failure as a part of the process. They set a lofty goal and put everything they had into achieving it, knowing full well that there was a chance they would fall short. And when they did fall short, they didn't shy away from it or try to hide it. Instead, they shared their journey with the world and used the experience to learn and improve.

This approach to failure is something that can be applied not just in business, but in life as well. Failure is not something to be ashamed of, but rather something to learn from and use to improve oneself. By taking risks and being willing to fail, we can push ourselves to new heights and achieve things we never thought possible.

On 12 October 2019, Kipchoge proved that with persistence anything is possible. 1:59:40. The project was a shining example of walking the walk and the importance of setting lofty targets,

Nike isn't a start-up and they have near unlimited resources but this is still a lesson in business, in innovation and in life.

Failure is not the end of the road. As long as we keep getting back up and pushing forward, failure is just a temporary setback on the road to success. So, don't be afraid to take risks and embrace failure as a necessary part of the journey. Who knows, you may just surprise yourself with what you're capable of achieving.

The Golden Rules

Throughout this book, I have shared my experiences and the lessons that I have learned through rugby, business, and life. I hope that these insights have been valuable to you and that you have found inspiration to apply them to your own journey.

As I conclude, I want to leave you with the Golden Rules that have guided me on and off the field. These rules are simple, yet powerful, and I have found them to be universally applicable in any situation.

The first rule is to go forward. No matter what obstacles you face, always move forward. Sometimes you may get knocked back, but that should not deter you from making progress. Take the next step.

The second rule is continuity. Once you have momentum, do whatever you can to maintain it. Keep doing what works, and don't let anything stop you.

The third rule is adaptability. Adapt and react to changing circumstances and situations. If it doesn't work, change it. Constantly develop and use your skill set to be creative in solving problems.

The fourth rule is communication. Be clear and transparent in your actions and intentions. Leave nothing to chance and share information. Let others know what you are doing and why. Be as willing to listen as you are open to speak.

The fifth rule is teamwork. No one can do it alone, always support and be honest with each other. You don't have to like one another but you do have to work together so put differences aside and focus on what needs to be done. Be constructive with criticism and don't take things personally, sometimes truths need to be told, but out and out negativity helps no one.

The final rule is to have fun. No matter what, have fun with what you are doing. After all, it's only a game, and there are more important things in life.

And lastly, always hang in there and keep going. Remember that this is just the beginning of your journey, and there will be challenges ahead. But with perseverance and dedication, you can achieve anything you set your mind to.

Thank you for joining me on this journey. I wish you all the best in your pursuits, and I hope that these Golden Rules will serve as a guide and inspiration for you.

The beginning.
KEEP GOING.